Contents

 Fiction

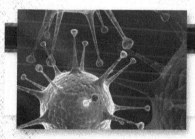

Non-fiction

Written by
David Grant

Illustrated by
Dylan Gibson
and **Andy Stephens**

Series editor **Dee Reid**

Heinemann
Part of Pearson

Characters

Jake

Kelly

Kris

Tricky words

- keyboards
- graveyard
- building
- brilliant

- groaned
- appeared
- panicked
- decided

Read these words to the student. Help them with these words when they appear in the text.

Introduction

Kris and Jake are best mates. Kelly is in their year at school. She is a computer genius. Most of the time, Kris and Jake get on well with Kelly but sometimes they are not sure about what she is up to on her computer. One day, Kris and Jake went round to Kelly's house. They were amazed at all her computer kit. Kris and Jake wanted to know if she could hack into someone's computer.

Kris and Jake went round to Kelly's house.
There were old computer screens, keyboards and
wires all over the place.
"Wow," said Kris as he looked around.
"It's like a graveyard for old computers," said Jake.

"And you've got two computers!" said Jake.
"This is my main computer," said Kelly. "And I just finished building this one. I'm testing it to see if it works."
"That's amazing," said Jake.
"I bet you can do all sorts of brilliant things on a computer, can't you?" said Kris.

"Yeah!" said Jake. "I bet you could hack into a bank."
"And steal loads of money," said Kris.
"Or you could hack into my sister's Facebook
and delete it," said Jake.
"Yeah! Let's do that!" said Kris.

"I could do that," said Kelly.
"Wow!" said Kris.
"Amazing!" said Jake.

"But I'm not going to," said Kelly.
"Oh!" groaned Kris and Jake.

"Why not?" asked Kris.

"You can get into really big trouble for hacking," said Kelly. "You can go to prison. Do you want me to get into trouble and go to prison?" Jake and Kris thought about it.

"I suppose not," said Kris. "But it would have been fun to try a bit of hacking."

"You don't have to be so clever to hack into someone's Facebook," said Jake. "You just need to work out the password. It's easy. Anyone can do it."
"I'm going to try it when I get home," said Kris.
"Me too," said Jake.
"Remember what I said," Kelly warned them.
But they weren't listening.

That evening, both Kris and Jake tried to hack into each other's Facebook accounts.

Kris spent ages trying to think of Jake's password. But each time he typed something he got the same message:
'The password you entered is incorrect. Please try again.'
Just as he was about to give up, Kris remembered that Jake loved sports cars.

Email:
Jake@mailnet.com

Password:
Ferrari

He typed 'Ferrari' as the password.
It worked!

Then suddenly a pop-up appeared on the screen:

WARNING!

Warning! You have been caught hacking into a Facebook account.
You are banned from using Facebook for life.
The police have been informed.

Done

Kris panicked.

Oh no! he thought. *Kelly said that you can get into big trouble for hacking. Why didn't I listen to her? What if the police come to my house? What will my mum say? I might go to prison! And I'll never be able to go on Facebook again!* He felt sick.

Just then his phone rang.
It was Jake.

Jake

"I'm in big trouble," said Jake. "I thought it
would be funny to hack into your
Facebook account but I've been caught!
I got a message that said I'm banned
from using Facebook for life. It also said
that the police had been informed!"
"I know," said Kris. "I did the same thing to you
and got the same message."

"What are we going to do? I'm really scared," said Jake.
"I don't know," said Kris. "I'm really scared too. I don't want to go to prison!"
Then suddenly, another pop-up appeared on their computer screens.

HA HA HA!

Ha ha ha! You wanted to hack into each other's Facebook page, so I decided to teach you both a lesson.
Next time, the warning might really be true and the police might be coming round to arrest you.
Kelly x

Done

So it was Kelly who had sent them both the warning message!
"I'm never going to try hacking again!" said Jake.
"Nor am I!" said Kris.

Kris checked his Facebook page, just to make sure he hadn't been banned.
He had a new friend request.
It was from Kelly!
Kris smiled and added Kelly as a friend.

Friend request
Kelly
Kelly has been added as a friend

Quiz ////////////////////////

Text comprehension

Literal comprehension
p5 What did Kris and Jake want Kelly to hack into?
p14–15 How did Kelly trick Kris and Jake?

Inferential comprehension
p7 Why is it funny when Kris and Jake have to think about it before saying they don't want Kelly to go to prison?
p14 Why do you think Kelly played the trick on Kris and Jake?
p15 Do you think Kris and Jake will try hacking again?

Personal response
- How would you feel if someone hacked into your Facebook account?
- Do you think it is right that hackers might go to prison?

Word knowledge

p3 What simile does Jake use?
p8 Find a word that means 'reminded'
p9 What is the punctuation after 'message'? Why is it used?

Spelling challenge

Read these words:

quickly   morning   important

Now try to spell them!

Ha! Ha! Ha!

What did the spider do on the computer?

Made a website!

Find out about

- How viruses can spread between computers and corrupt data.

Tricky words

- attachments
- hoaxes
- programmed
- released

- suspended
- committed
- sentenced
- expensive

Read these words to the student. Help them with these words when they appear in the text.

Introduction

A computer virus moves from computer to computer. It might damage the computer and it can even delete everything on it. Some viruses are sent in attachments to emails. Computer viruses are often created by teenage boys but they are also the people who create programs to stop viruses.

Viruses Attack!

Computer viruses

A human virus moves from person
to person, making them ill.
A computer virus moves from computer
to computer.
It might damage the computer and it
can even delete everything on it.

Spreading computer viruses

Some viruses are spread in attachments to emails. You might get an email which warns of a new and deadly computer virus.
But watch out!
Most of these warnings are hoaxes.

Worse still, the email might actually carry
a virus. If you open the attachment, your
computer will get it!
The hoax email asks you to send the message
on to everyone you know.
But if you do send it on, you will just spread
the virus to all your contacts.

Why do people send emails like this?
Perhaps they think it is a joke to damage lots of people's computers.
Or perhaps the sender wants to see
how far their message will spread.

The first computer virus

The first ever computer virus was created in 1982
by a 15-year-old American boy.
The virus was harmless compared to viruses today.
It moved from computer to computer when
a disc was copied.
Every 50th time it was copied, a poem would
pop up on the screen!

Deadly viruses

In 2003, a virus called Blaster began to attack computers.

It spread itself using the internet and was programmed to send thousands of messages to the Microsoft website and make it crash.

A message to the chairman of Microsoft, Bill Gates, was hidden in the computer code. It said: 'Bill Gates, why do you make this possible? Stop making money and fix your software!'

In 2004, an 18 year old called Sven released the Sasser virus onto the internet. It was a deadly virus.
It attacked Microsoft computers and stopped them working before sending itself on to other Microsoft computers using the internet.

Microsoft offered a big reward of $250,000 for any information about the person who had created this virus. Lots of people wanted the reward and they gave information which meant Microsoft could find Sven.

Sven was given a suspended sentence of 21 months. This meant that he would not go to prison unless he committed another crime.

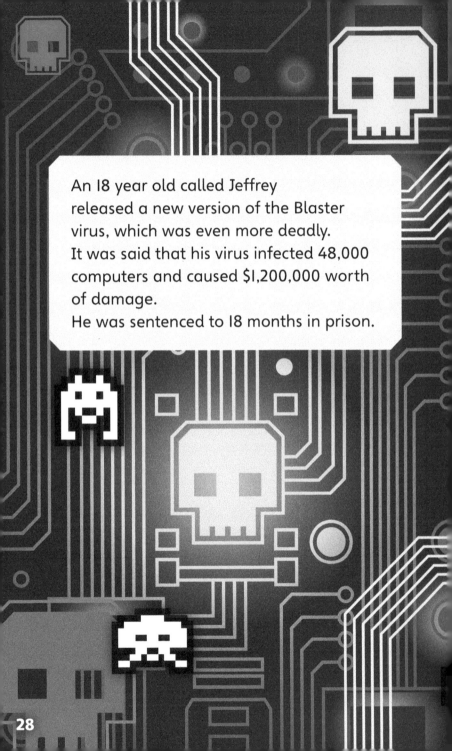

An 18 year old called Jeffrey
released a new version of the Blaster
virus, which was even more deadly.
It was said that his virus infected 48,000
computers and caused $1,200,000 worth
of damage.
He was sentenced to 18 months in prison.

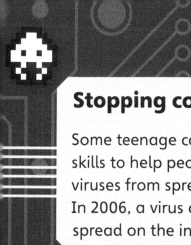

Stopping computer viruses

Some teenage computer experts use their skills to help people and stop computer viruses from spreading.
In 2006, a virus called Sgrunt began to spread on the internet.

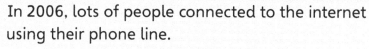

In 2006, lots of people connected to the internet using their phone line.
The Sgrunt program used your computer to dial expensive phone numbers while you were connected to the internet.
The owners of those phone numbers made lots of money and you got a large phone bill.

But then a 13-year-old boy called Francesco created a program which stopped the virus. The program was called KillSgrunt. More than 45,000 copies of it were downloaded from his website.

Francesco did not charge any money for the program.
But he did ask people to give some money to charity.
Lots of computer companies were amazed at
how clever Francesco had been to stop the virus
and they asked him to come and work for them.
But Francesco would not work for any of them.
He told them: "I'm just a child."

Teenagers have often been the ones to create
the viruses that attack computers.
But they have also been the ones to stop them!

Quiz ////////////////////////

Text comprehension

Literal comprehension
p20 Why should you be careful if you get an email warning of a virus?

p27 How did Microsoft track down Sven?

Inferential comprehension
p23 Why was the first computer virus not harmful?

p25 Why would the Blaster virus send that message to Bill Gates?

p30 How do we know Francesco's program was popular?

Personal response
- Why do you think it is usually teenage boys who create and crack viruses?
- Have you ever had a virus on your computer?

Word knowledge

p20 Find two adjectives on this page.

p22 Find a word that means 'spoil'.

p23 Find a word that means the opposite of 'harmful'.

Spelling challenge

Read these words:

using   meant   clever

Now write them from memory!

Ha! Ha! Ha!

Why did the computer sneeze?

It had a virus!